Laurence King Publishing Ltd
361—373 City Road, London EC1V 1LR, United Kingdom
www.laurenceking.com

Magma for Laurence King

© text 2015 Aaron Tan
© illustrations 2015 Holly Exley

Design & Art Direction: Atlas

ISBN: 978-1-85669-978-5

Printed in China

Contents

FOR YOUR OWN RECIPES, REVIEWS AND CLIPPINGS

Recipes

Café / Patisserie Reviews

Labels & Souvenirs

Useful Information

COUNTRY:

PREPARATION TIME:

COOKING TIME:

SERVES:
② ④ ⑥ ⑧

DIFFICULTY:
○ ○ ○ ○ ○

INGREDIENTS:

RECIPE:

PREPARATION:

COUNTRY:

RECIPE:

PREPARATION:

PREPARATION TIME:

COOKING TIME:

SERVES:

② ④ ⑥ ⑧

DIFFICULTY:

○ ○ ○ ○ ○

INGREDIENTS:

COUNTRY:

RECIPE:

PREPARATION:

PREPARATION TIME:

COOKING TIME:

SERVES:

② ④ ⑥ ⑧

DIFFICULTY:

○ ○ ○ ○ ○

INGREDIENTS:

COUNTRY:

RECIPE:

PREPARATION:

PREPARATION TIME:

COOKING TIME:

SERVES:

② ④ ⑥ ⑧

DIFFICULTY:

○ ○ ○ ○ ○

INGREDIENTS:

COUNTRY:

RECIPE:

PREPARATION:

PREPARATION TIME:

COOKING TIME:

SERVES:

② ④ ⑥ ⑧

DIFFICULTY:

○ ○ ○ ○ ○

INGREDIENTS:

COUNTRY:

RECIPE:

PREPARATION:

PREPARATION TIME:

COOKING TIME:

SERVES:
② ④ ⑥ ⑧

DIFFICULTY:
○ ○ ○ ○ ○

INGREDIENTS:

COUNTRY:

RECIPE:

PREPARATION:

PREPARATION TIME:

COOKING TIME:

SERVES:

② ④ ⑥ ⑧

DIFFICULTY:

○ ○ ○ ○ ○

INGREDIENTS:

COUNTRY:

RECIPE:

PREPARATION:

PREPARATION TIME:

COOKING TIME:

SERVES:

② ④ ⑥ ⑧

DIFFICULTY:

○ ○ ○ ○ ○

INGREDIENTS:

COUNTRY:

RECIPE:

PREPARATION:

PREPARATION TIME:

COOKING TIME:

SERVES:

② ④ ⑥ ⑧

DIFFICULTY:

○ ○ ○ ○ ○

INGREDIENTS:

COUNTRY:

RECIPE:

PREPARATION:

PREPARATION TIME:

COOKING TIME:

SERVES:

② ④ ⑥ ⑧

DIFFICULTY:

○ ○ ○ ○ ○

INGREDIENTS:

CAFÉ / PATISSERIE:

ADDRESS:

PRICE:

QUALITY: ☆ ☆ ☆ ☆ ☆

REVIEW:

_____

_____

_____

_____

_____

_____

_____

_____

_____

BUSINESS CARD

CAFÉ / PATISSERIE:

ADDRESS:

PRICE:

QUALITY: ☆ ☆ ☆ ☆ ☆

REVIEW:

_____

_____

_____

_____

_____

_____

_____

_____

_____

BUSINESS CARD

CAFÉ / PATISSERIE:

ADDRESS:

PRICE:

QUALITY: ☆ ☆ ☆ ☆ ☆

REVIEW:

BUSINESS CARD

CAFÉ / PATISSERIE:

ADDRESS:

PRICE:

QUALITY: ☆ ☆ ☆ ☆ ☆

REVIEW:

BUSINESS CARD

CAFÉ / PATISSERIE:

ADDRESS:

PRICE:

QUALITY: ☆ ☆ ☆ ☆ ☆

REVIEW:

BUSINESS CARD

CAFÉ / PATISSERIE:

ADDRESS:

PRICE:

QUALITY: ☆ ☆ ☆ ☆ ☆

REVIEW:

BUSINESS CARD

CAFÉ / PATISSERIE: | ADDRESS:

PRICE:

QUALITY: ☆ ☆ ☆ ☆ ☆

REVIEW:

_____

_____

_____

_____

_____

_____

_____

_____

_____

_____

BUSINESS CARD

CAFÉ / PATISSERIE: | ADDRESS:

PRICE:

QUALITY: ☆ ☆ ☆ ☆ ☆

REVIEW:

_____

_____

_____

_____

_____

_____

_____

_____

_____

_____

BUSINESS CARD

CAFÉ / PATISSERIE:

ADDRESS:

PRICE:

QUALITY: ☆ ☆ ☆ ☆ ☆

REVIEW:

_____

_____

_____

_____

_____

_____

_____

_____

_____

_____

BUSINESS CARD

CAFÉ / PATISSERIE:

ADDRESS:

PRICE:

QUALITY: ☆ ☆ ☆ ☆ ☆

REVIEW:

_____

_____

_____

_____

_____

_____

_____

_____

_____

_____

BUSINESS CARD

CAFÉ / PATISSERIE:

ADDRESS:

PRICE:

QUALITY: ☆ ☆ ☆ ☆ ☆

REVIEW:

_____
_____
_____
_____
_____
_____
_____
_____
_____
_____
_____

BUSINESS CARD

CAFÉ / PATISSERIE:

ADDRESS:

PRICE:

QUALITY: ☆ ☆ ☆ ☆ ☆

REVIEW:

_____
_____
_____
_____
_____
_____
_____
_____
_____
_____
_____

BUSINESS CARD

CAFÉ / PATISSERIE:

ADDRESS:

PRICE:

QUALITY: ☆ ☆ ☆ ☆ ☆

REVIEW:

BUSINESS CARD

CAFÉ / PATISSERIE:

ADDRESS:

PRICE:

QUALITY: ☆ ☆ ☆ ☆ ☆

REVIEW:

BUSINESS CARD

CAFÉ / PATISSERIE:

ADDRESS:

PRICE:

QUALITY: ☆ ☆ ☆ ☆ ☆

REVIEW:

_____
_____
_____
_____
_____
_____
_____
_____
_____
_____
_____

BUSINESS CARD

CAFÉ / PATISSERIE:

ADDRESS:

PRICE:

QUALITY: ☆ ☆ ☆ ☆ ☆

REVIEW:

_____
_____
_____
_____
_____
_____
_____
_____
_____
_____
_____

BUSINESS CARD

CAFÉ / PATISSERIE:

ADDRESS:

PRICE:

QUALITY: ☆ ☆ ☆ ☆ ☆

BUSINESS CARD

REVIEW:

_____
_____
_____
_____
_____
_____
_____
_____
_____

CAFÉ / PATISSERIE:

ADDRESS:

PRICE:

QUALITY: ☆ ☆ ☆ ☆ ☆

BUSINESS CARD

REVIEW:

_____
_____
_____
_____
_____
_____
_____
_____
_____

CAFÉ / PATISSERIE:

ADDRESS:

PRICE:

QUALITY: ☆☆☆☆☆

REVIEW:

_____

_____

_____

_____

_____

_____

_____

_____

_____

_____

_____

_____

BUSINESS CARD

CAFÉ / PATISSERIE:

ADDRESS:

PRICE:

QUALITY: ☆☆☆☆☆

REVIEW:

_____

_____

_____

_____

_____

_____

_____

_____

_____

_____

_____

_____

BUSINESS CARD

LABELS, NAPKINS, BILLS/CHECKS FROM CAFÉS AND PATISSERIES, AND OTHER SOUVENIRS

LABELS, NAPKINS, BILLS/CHECKS FROM CAFÉS AND PATISSERIES, AND OTHER SOUVENIRS

LABELS, NAPKINS, BILLS/CHECKS FROM CAFÉS AND PATISSERIES, AND OTHER SOUVENIRS

LABELS, NAPKINS, BILLS/CHECKS FROM CAFÉS AND PATISSERIES, AND OTHER SOUVENIRS

Useful Information

The Origins of Baking

The prehistoric discoveries of fire-making and grains are said to have produced the first rudimentary baked good, which has been likened to a modern unleavened flat bread. The development of baking as we know it today is credited to the ancient Mediterranean civilizations of Egypt and Greece, and really flourished as an artisan form with the Romans. In parallel with the expansion of the empire, baking spread to other parts of Europe and Asia. Indeed, the history of baking can be tracked alongside the rise and fall of empires, colonial expansion and the evolutions that have shaped the world.

Britain
13 century. First reference to Cornish pasty.
18-19th century. Sieves made from Chinese silks produced finer, whiter flour, which led to the rise of white bread.
1843. Chemist Alfred Bird invented the first modern baking power.

France
1787-89. Bread riots fuelled the French Revolution.
1803. Marie Carème, father of modern pastry and French cooking, opened his pastry shop.

Portugal
16th century. Colonial traders brought chocolate back to Europe from the New World. It was consumed as a beverage until the industrial revolution, when the first solid chocolate was developed and used for baking.

Rome
c. 150 BC. First baker's guild was formed.
c. 500 BC. The circular quern was developed. It is still used today to grind flour.
c. 1 AD. More than 300 pastry chefs in Rome.

Poland
16th century. The bagel was invented and became a staple in the Slavic diet.

Austria
1839. The croissant was invented.

Greece
c. 500 BC. The first front-loaded oven was created (prototype for the wood-fire oven of today).
c. 450 BC. The watermill was invented.
c. 400 BC. Aristophanes wrote about honey flanes patterned to tortes and doughnut-like bread called dispyrus.

Egypt
c. 4000 BC. Yeast was used to brew beer and leaven bread.
c. 3000 BC. Pyramid builders were paid with bread.

Leavening Agents

A leavening agent (sometimes called a raising or rising agent, leavening or leaven) is a substance used in doughs and batters to cause them to rise, making the finished product softer and lighter. Leavening agents react with moisture, heat, acidity or other triggers to produce gas (often carbon dioxide) that becomes trapped as bubbles within the dough or batter.

Live Leavening Agents

BAKERS' YEAST A commercially produced single-celled fungus (S. cerevisiae) which is used in baked goods as a leavening agent. When provided with the right conditions (moisture, heat, food and time), the live yeast feeds on the sugars in the dough, converting it into alcohol and carbon dioxide. It is the carbon dioxide trapped in the dough that makes it rise, while the alcohol evaporates in the oven. There are three main types of bakers' yeast: fresh yeast, dried active (active dry) yeast and fast-action (instant) yeast.

FRESH YEAST Favoured by artisan bakers, who swear by its stability, flavour and superior rising ability. It can be crumbled directly into your dry ingredients or softened in tepid water first. Considered to be the most active type of yeast, it is also the most perishable (it lasts for two weeks when refrigerated). It can also be frozen, but remember to portion it out before freezing.

DRIED ACTIVE (ACTIVE DRY) YEAST As its name suggests, this is yeast that has been dried but contains active cells. It comes in granular form with a protective layer of dead yeast debris. When it comes into contact with water, the protective layer dissolves and the dormant live cells are activated. Thus, it has to be rehydrated in warm water (about 43°C/110°F is considered optimal) for about 10 minutes before being added to the dough.

FAST-ACTION (INSTANT) YEAST Often confused with dried active (active dry) yeast, and sold under myriad names, such as 'quick rise', 'fast-acting', 'rapid rise', 'easy blend' and 'bread machine' yeast. There are three main differences between them, however. Fast-action yeast has a layer of dead cells that is thinner than dried active yeast, so it can be added to the dough directly, without rehydration. Fast-action yeast comes in a finer granular form, and is also more concentrated and active, which means it requires a shorter proving (proofing) time. Thus, when converting dried active to fast-action yeast, use three-quarters of the amount called for.

SOURDOUGH STARTER Essentially a fermented mixture of flour and water that harnesses the power of wild yeasts and bacteria in the environment. When flour and water are mixed, the enzymes in the flour break the starch down into sugar that is food for the hungry swarms of yeasts and bacteria that surround us. Unlike monocultural bakers' yeast, a sourdough starter is an ecosystem inhabited by different types of wild yeasts and bacteria. This results in a biodiversity that gives each sourdough loaf its individuality and resilience. If nurtured properly, a starter can be passed down through generations! In contrast with the homogeneity of bakers' yeast, the different strains of wild yeast in a sourdough starter produce carbon dioxide at varying rates, so there is no average or uniform leavening rate when using sourdough starters.

Chemical Leavening Agents

BAKING POWDER A raising agent made from alkaline bicarbonate of soda (baking soda), acidic cream of tartar and a drying agent such as cornflour (cornstarch), which is needed so that a chemical reaction does not take place before a liquid is added. Unlike live yeast, there is no fermentation, but rather a chemical reaction when the baking powder is added to the batter and comes in contact with moisture. The acid reacts with the alkaline and starts to produce carbon dioxide immediately. Most baking powder used today is 'double acting', which means a second rise happens when the mixture is exposed to the blast of heat in the oven. This means that the time elapsed between mixing and baking is less critical than when using 'single acting' types, or bicarbonate of soda (baking soda).

BICARBONATE OF SODA (BAKING SODA) A chemical leavening agent that can be found in baking powder. Since it is an alkaline compound, it is activated with the aid of an acid and moisture. It is therefore used in recipes alongside acidic ingredients such as sour cream, buttermilk, citrus juice, chocolate and honey. The resulting chemical reaction produces bubbles of carbon dioxide that aerate mixtures and give it rise.

The reaction happens immediately, and the dough or batter therefore needs to be baked as soon as possible, otherwise you risk an end result that literally falls flat.

CREAM OF TARTAR A by-product of winemaking, used to stabilize egg whites or cream while whipping them. It also used as an acid ingredient to activate bicarbonate of soda (baking soda) in baking powder.

Mechanical Leavening Agents

AIR AND WATER The unsung heroes of the leavening world are simply the air and/or water that are incorporated into the dough during mixing, whipping or other mechanical means. Whisking egg whites to stiff peaks perfectly illustrates the importance of air in creating dramatic volume, especially since the former retains its expanded structure after baking.

Flour

Flour for baking is mainly made by grinding wheat, although it can also be milled from corn, rice and other starches. Wheat flour, by far the most popular and versatile flour, is made up of starch, protein and, in the case of wholemeal (whole-wheat) flour, fat. Of the three main constituents of wheat flour, protein matters most to the baker. Different countries process and label their flours differently, so it is helpful to know the characteristics and purposes of the main varieties.

Glutenous Flour

PLAIN (ALL-PURPOSE) WHITE FLOUR A blend of flours with high and low protein levels, all of which are milled from the endosperm of the wheat grain. It is used for general baking because of its average protein content of 8—11%. Confusingly, flours that are bleached naturally are marketed as 'unbleached' and have a higher protein level than the chemically treated 'bleached' types (which are not permitted in the UK). Natural bleaching enhances the flour's gluten-forming potential, but because the process is time-consuming, chemicals are added to simulate it, although the flavour and nutritional value are compromised as a result.

SELF-RAISING (SELF-RISING) FLOUR Plain (all-purpose) white flour to which a leavening agent, usually baking powder, and salt have been added. To make your own, add 1½ teaspoons baking powder and ¼ teaspoon of salt to 125 g/1 cup plain (all-purpose) white flour.

CAKE OR PASTRY FLOUR Lower-protein flours sometimes called for in American recipes, but not easily found in other parts of the world. Cake flour typically has a 6—8% protein content and pastry flour has a 8.5—9.5% protein content. Both are milled from softer (lower-protein) wheat varieties and they are finer than plain (all-purpose) white flour. Use 125 g/1 cup plain (all-purpose) white flour, substituting 2 tablespoons of it for cornflour (cornstarch), as a substitute for cake flour. Sift to combine the flours before using.

STRONG BREAD FLOUR Milled from hard wheat, this flour is best used for bread because of its high protein levels (11—15%), which enhances its gluten elasticity. It is excellent for yeasted bread making and comes in white or wholemeal (whole-wheat) varieties.

WHOLEMEAL (WHOLE-WHEAT) FLOUR This is made from the whole kernel of the grain and as a result has a higher fat content, along with higher fibre and more nutritional content than white flours. It should be stored in the refrigerator to prevent the oils in the flour from turning rancid. It is also denser than white flour and absorbs more water, which means that the dough requires more kneading for a good rise.

GRANARY (MALTED) BREAD FLOUR This is usually white flour with added flakes of malted grains. Malting is a process in which grains such as wheat, barley or rye are left to sprout. When added to dough, enzymes in the flour convert starch into maltose (a type of sugar). The maltose provides more food for yeast production, giving more flavour and colour to the end product.

RYE FLOUR Rye is a grain similar to wheat and barley and its flour is used to produce dense and dark bread, or is mixed with wheat flour for a lighter loaf. Rye flour contains the same amount of protein as wheat flour, but its proteins have little leavening effect, resulting in a dense, sticky dough that takes longer to rise. It is prized for its intense, complex flavour, often enhanced with the addition of molasses and caraway seeds.

SPELT FLOUR An ancient grain that is a relative to common wheat, spelt has received renewed interest from specialty bakers and health-conscious consumers. The delicate, water-soluble gluten in spelt flour means it is easier to digest than wheat flour, but is trickier to bake with. Over-mixing or heating can cause the gluten to break down and the dough to spread out, and water should be added with care (reduce the water called for in wheat flour recipes). Spelt flour lends a dense and

flavoursome result to breads and biscuits (cookies).

Gluten-Free Flour

Gluten-free flours cannot be used to make yeasted baked goods on their own, but are sometimes added to wheat flour to add flavour, nutrition and a denser consistency.

RICE FLOUR Also known as rice powder or ground rice, rice flour comes in different varieties including white, brown and glutinous. In the West, it is used as an alternative to wheat flours in cakes and biscuits (cookies), and gives a grainy texture to the latter. In Asia, glutinous rice flour is a common

ingredient in the kitchen, such as in the sweet and savoury bite-sized cakes known as kuih.

OAT FLOUR This is a gluten-free form of whole-grain flour made from whole oats. It has a high nutritional content and gives baked goods a chewy and crumbly texture and a sweet and nutty flavour. Do note that oats are often grown or processed alongside wheat, barley or rye and thus may be contaminated with gluten. Always check that the packaging states that the flour is indeed gluten-free.

BUCKWHEAT FLOUR Despite its name, buckwheat flour is not derived from wheat and does not contain any gluten. It is often blended with other gluten-free flours for gluten-free baking.

Fats

Fats, whether butter, margarine, vegetable shortening, oil, lard or suet, have the ability to tenderize the baked product by coating and weakening the gluten bonds within the structure. The result of this can be seen in the fine-grained texture of a cake as opposed to the chewy, gluten-rich texture of a low-fat bread. Fats add moisture to the baked product as they don't evaporate like water, and also move heat around efficiently, thus aiding the baking process.

BUTTER Produced when milk or cream are churned until the fats separate from the liquid (known as buttermilk). Thus, butter is made up of milk fat with water and other milk solids. In the US, butter must contain at least 80% milk fat, whereas its European counterpart has a slightly higher fat content. Butter is prized for its superior flavour and gives a wonderful 'melt-in-the-mouth' sensation. This sensation can be attributed to butter's melting point, which is just below the body temperature,

so it melts very nicely in the mouth. Butter is sold unsalted and salted; unsalted is generally preferred in baking as it allows the baker to control the salt content.

MARGARINE Invented in the 1860s under a Napoleonic directive for a butter substitute. It has a similar composition to butter (at least 80% fat), but is often derived from hydrogenated or refined plant oils with milk products added to it. For a long time margarine was considered to be a healthier option than butter, but news of its trans-fatty acids (a by-product of hydrogenation) has diminished this reputation. Do take care and read the label when substituting it for butter, as there are 'light' versions that are only good for spreading on bread. You can also check if the product is suitable for use in baking if one tablespoon yields 100 calories. Commercially, it is often used as an ingredient in puff pastry and cookies.

VEGETABLE SHORTENING Like margarine, vegetable shortening is vegetable oil that has been hydrogenated, a process by which oil can be made solid at room temperature. It is, however, 100% fat, unlike margarine or butter. Shortening is useful in baking because it can help make the pastry or crust tender and flaky by preventing the cohesion of wheat gluten, making the gluten strands shorter (hence its name). Like butter, it can be creamed and because of its high melting point, it can hold the structure of a baked good at a higher temperature. If substituting shortening for margarine or butter, increase the liquid quantity slightly, as vegetable shortening has no water content at all.

OIL Vegetable oils that are obtained from nuts, seeds or vegetables are 100% fat and remain liquid at room temperature. The different types of vegetable oils, such as soya bean, coconut, corn, peanut (groundnut) and sunflower, vary greatly in their percentage of saturated fat. For baking and health purposes, choose an oil that has a high percentage of polyunsaturated and/or monounsaturated fats, such as olive, soybean, safflower or corn oil. The use of olive oil is usually suggested for bread and rolls rather than cakes because of its strong flavour. The liquid consistency of vegetable oil helps add moisture and tenderize the mixture but will not give any structure to the baked product, unlike vegetable shortening. It should also not be used in a recipe that calls for creaming. When replacing butter with oil, follow the principle that oil is 100% fat, whereas butter is roughly 80%

fat and 18% water; thus you will need to use 80% of the weight of butter as oil and compensate for the water content with milk or sour cream.

LARD This has always been an important baking staple in cultures where pork is consumed. The best lard, 'leaf lard', is obtained from the fat around the pig's kidney, but industrially produced lard is rendered from a mixture of fats of varying quality found throughout the pig, and is hydrogenated for longer shelf life. Like vegetable oil and shortening, it is 100% fat. Lard has a large crystalline structure and a high melting point, which makes it extremely effective as a

shortening for flaky pie crusts and biscuits (cookies), but will not work as well in fine-grained cakes.

SUET The equivalent of leaf lard, except that it comes from cows and sheep. It is used in traditional English steamed and baked puddings such as the sweet spotted dick and the savoury steak-and-kidney pudding. Suet's high melting point means that it does not fully integrate with the pastry dough and melts only after it has set, giving the dough a puffy lightness as well as flavour. Suet is becoming quite hard to source, especially in America, where it is not comonly used. Try asking your local butcher.

Tips: Ingredients

When separating egg whites, use one bowl to catch each white and then transfer it to another. This prevents spoiling a bowl of whites if a little bit of yolk falls in. If this happens, use a piece of eggshell to remove the stray yolk.

If a recipe calls only for egg yolks, freeze the whites in ice-cube trays; they will be as good as new when defrosted overnight.

To check the freshness of eggs, put them in a bowl of water. If they sink, they're fresh. If they sit upright on the bottom, they are not. Discard any eggs that float right to the top.

If a recipe does not specify a size, use large eggs (extra-large in the US). Always use room-temperature eggs unless stated otherwise. You can warm cold eggs in a bowl of hot water for 10 minutes.

Re-use your butter wrappers for greasing the sides of your cake tin (pan).

If possible, weigh flour rather than measuring it in cups, for accuracy.

If using store-bought gluten-free flour, try replacing some with ground almonds (almond meal) to give a moist, nutty texture. This will work especially well with pastries, biscuits (cookies), and denser cakes and breads. Note that nut flours cook quicker and therefore burn easily, so you will need to adjust the oven temperature and baking time.

Keep wholemeal (whole-wheat) flour in a tightly sealed container in the refrigerator or freezer to prevent rancidity from the natural oils present in the wheat germ. A bay leaf in the flour canister will keep the bugs away.

A pinch of salt brings out the flavour of sweet baked goods, but too much can inhibit yeast formation.

Check the strength of your baking powder by mixing 1 teaspoon with 80 ml ($1/3$ cup) boiling water; it should bubble up violently. For bicarbonate of soda (baking soda), add a few drops of vinegar or lemon juice to a pinch of the powder. It should bubble over too.

Use the heaviest-gauge metal pot you have when making caramel, as this distributes heat evenly. Avoid using non-stick pans, as the high heat can release toxic compounds.

Use refined granulated sugar when making caramel, as other types may contain impurities that can impede the process.

Use caster (superfine) sugar in cakes rather than granulated, as it dissolves more easily.

Bread Techniques

Kneading

Kneading a bread dough helps develop and strengthen the gluten while distributing the gas pockets produced by the yeast. It can either be done by hand or by a mixer. Over-kneading or under-kneading the dough will result in dense bread — do the windowpane test if in doubt (see Bread Tips). Flour or oil is used to aid the kneading by preventing sticking, but because flour alters the moisture levels of the dough, oil is preferred. Leave the dough to rest for 10 minutes after mixing; this will help it lose some of its initial stickiness and reduce the need to add flour.

1. Coat a clean work counter lightly with oil. Add more oil to the dough and on your hands and proceed to scrape the dough out from the bowl onto the counter. Wash and oil the inside of the bowl, as you will need it later.

2. With the heel of your dominant hand, push the dough down and out, stretching it flat away from you and return it back to fold it. Your other hand will hold the dough in place. This action will serve to lengthen the gluten strands in the dough.

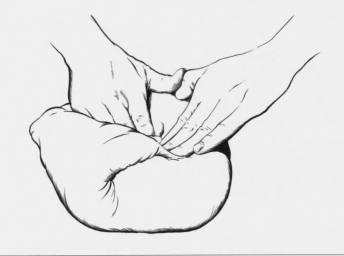

3. Lift and rotate the dough about a quarter turn. Repeat the pressing, stretching, folding and rotating action about 10 more times. If the dough starts to stick to the counter during this time, add more oil. Pick the dough up and flip it back into the oiled bowl, then cover with a cloth and let it rest for 10 minutes.

4. Repeat the kneading procedure twice more at 10-minute intervals, and you should end up with dough that is smooth, silky and supple.

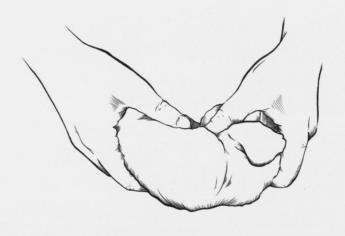

Bread Tips

To check if your dough has been sufficiently kneaded, use the windowpane test. Pinch off a small chunk of dough and stretch it out from the four corners. If it forms a translucent membrane without breaking, the gluten networks are well developed and the dough is ready.

Test to see if dried yeast is still active by adding 1 teaspoon sugar and 2 teaspoons yeast (or 1 packet) to half a cup of warm water. If foam and bubbles appear within 10 minutes, the yeast is still active.

Cake Techniques

Creaming

The creaming technique emulsifies sugar and a solid fat, usually butter, through vigorous mixing to form a pale and fluffy mixture. This can be done with a wooden spoon (and a lot of elbow grease) or with an electric mixer. Air pockets are formed when the sugar crystals puncture the fat molecules in the butter, which adds volume to the mixture. Eggs are usually added afterwards to give body, and then flour for structure. Ensure that all ingredients are at room temperature before creaming.

Whisking/Whipping

Whisking is the process of incorporating air into ingredients such as egg whites, whole eggs or double (heavy) cream to increase the volume and achieve the desired consistency of the mixture. It is done with a balloon whisk or an electric whisk. When whisking egg whites, it is critical that they have not retained any of the yolk or been in contact with a greasy substance, as this can impede the whites from expanding. They should also be at room temperature, and should be whisked in a large, clean and dry bowl. When whisking by hand, start with small strokes in a steady rhythm and gradually pick up speed with larger strokes. At no point should you stop whisking, as this will cause the whites to disintegrate. If a recipe calls for soft peaks, turn your whisk upside down and the peaks should begin to hold but collapse after a second. For stiff peaks, the peaks will stay upright without folding back on themselves and the mixture will be thick and firm. You can double check by holding the bowl upside-down. If the mixture stays in the bowl, you are good to go.

Rubbing In

Rubbing in is a method of coating flour with a solid fat by rubbing the fat until it combines with the flour to form a breadcrumb-like mixture. Working the fat into the dough stops the gluten strands in the flour from lengthening and produces a crumbly texture ideal for shortcrust pastry (basic pie dough), scones, shortbread and biscuits (cookies).

Folding

Folding involves gently incorporating a light, aerated mixture into a heavier mixture so as to retain as much air as possible. The lighter mixture (such as whisked egg whites or whipped cream) is usually added to the heavier one and is combined by passing a spatula down through the mixture, scooping from the bottom, drawing it up and folding it over. Repeat the folding action with a partial turn of the bowl so that the two mixtures are lightly and evenly combined. This technique is not to be confused with the folding involved in bread making.

Piping

1. Make the icing (frosting) with a good firm consistency. Prepare a piping (pastry) bag with a nozzle (tip). Fill the bag by placing it in a tall drinking glass and fold the excess down over the glass. Using a spatula, fill the bag with the icing (frosting) or other contents, pressing down gently each time and packing it down to remove any air bubbles.

2. Fill the bag halfway and unfold it from the glass. Push all the contents down towards the nozzle (tip) and tighten the end with a twist. Hold the twisted end of the bag between the thumb and your index finger and squeeze some of the contents back into the bowl to get rid of any remaining air pockets.

3. With your dominant hand still grasping the twisted end of the bag, use the other hand to support the nozzle (tip) end of the bag. This will give you stability as you pipe. Alternatively, you could also anchor the piping hand with your other hand.

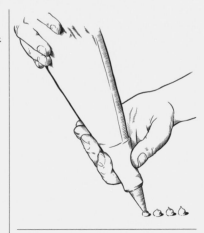

4. You are now ready to pipe. For dots or swirls, hold the bag vertically with the nozzle (tip) close to the surface and squeeze gently from the top of the bag. To finish, stop squeezing as you push down gently and draw up sharply. This will give a nice clean finish. When piping choux pastry or meringue, take care not to touch the nozzle (tip) to the baking paper or you will lose volume.

Cake Tips

Make sure all the ingredients are at room temperature, for a cold cake batter will not trap air bubbles efficiently for a good rise.

To make a fluffier cake, substitute some of the flour with cornflour (cornstarch). As a gauge, replace 2 tablespoons of flour for every 250 g (2 cups).

When baking cakes, sift the flour before use, as this will incorporate air and yield an airy cake. Also, do not over-beat the flour into the batter; simply stir or fold it in until the flour is incorporated.

To prevent fruit and chocolate from sinking to the bottom of the cake, make sure the cake batter is not too runny, and the fruit has as little moisture as possible. Adding more flour can stiffen up the cake mixture.

To tell if a cake is done, insert a fine skewer into the centre; it should come out clean.

Let cakes cool down before cutting, filling or decorating. This allows the moisture to escape and the proteins to set.

To prevent a filling from oozing, create an icing or frosting dam by piping a ring around the bottom layer. Refrigerate until set, then spread with the filling.

A crumb coat is a thinned mixture of the icing or frosting that is used to cover the surface of the cake, which, when set, will seal the cake for a second round of perfect crumb-free icing or frosting. Alternatively, apricot jam can be used.

Slice cakes with a sturdy serrated knife to ensure a clean cut. For a perfectly level cake, trim the top off evenly and then flip it to create a flat surface ready for icing.

Pastry Techniques

Pastry is basically a dough or paste primarily constituted of flour, water and fat, and used for both sweet and savoury baked goods. Its high fat and low gluten content distinguishes it from bread doughs and produces a crumbly or flaky texture that is enjoyed in many parts of the world. The American category of 'cookie' includes what in the UK are called 'biscuits' and 'cookies'; the latter have a softer, chewier centre and are often larger and richer. Confusingly, the American 'biscuit' is similar to the UK scone.

Shortcrust Pastry (Basic Pie Dough)

Shortcrust pastry (basic pie dough) and its sweetened variation, sweet pastry or pâte sucrée, bake to a wonderfully compact and crumbly texture, which makes them ideal as receptacles for fruits, custards, meats and other fillings. They are often made with a half-fat, half-flour ratio using the rubbing-in or creaming techniques. The old adage that cold hands make good pastry rings true here: if the fat gets too warm, it will require more flour and you will end up with a tougher pastry. This is also why most recipes call for the fat, and even the flour, to be chilled beforehand. To achieve a soft, tender pastry, work quickly to coat the flour with fat to minimize heat transference and prevent gluten strands from developing. A food processor will be useful for this purpose. Cold water is usually added to bind mixture together, and the dough is chilled briefly to allow the gluten that has developed to relax, making it easier to roll out.

Filo (Phyllo) Pastry

Filo (phyllo) pastry is a tissue-thin pastry that is often layered in sheets and then baked to a flaky and delicate texture. It is used in Greek, Middle Eastern and eastern European cuisines, and has the reputation of being the most difficult pastry to make, as both skill and time are needed to achieve the required thinness. The dough is made with just flour, water, salt and oil, and each sheet is brushed with oil or melted butter before being layered with another. This serves as a glue to bond the sheets and when baked, they rise and separate as steam is released, resulting in a flaky layered pastry. When using filo (phyllo) pastry, keep the sheets moist by covering them with a kitchen cloth, as they dry out very easily.

Puff Pastry

Puff pastry is said to have derived from filo (phyllo) pastry, and indeed they look similar in their final baked form. However, it is the continuous folding and rolling out of the dough with a rectangular sheet of solid fat that gives puff pastry its rich, multi-layered form. When the dough is baked, thin layers of butter trapped between the sheets of dough melt and prevent the steam in the dough from escaping, which inflates the pastry as a result. The basic ingredients are flour, butter, water and salt. Croissant dough is a yeast-leavened version of puff pastry (milk and sugar are also added). Other variations include rough puff and flaky pastry, in which chunks of fat are coarsely rubbed in with the flour, making it less time-consuming for the baker.

In the case of flaky pastry, more chunks of fat are added to the rolled-out dough. They are called for in recipes where the need for a flaky texture outweighs that for a good rise, such as in savoury pies and pasties.

Choux Pastry (Paste)

Choux pastry (paste) is distinctive because it is pre-cooked before being baked, and the dough is so soft that it needs to be spooned or piped. It is made by first melting fat in water and/or milk, which is then brought to a boil. Flour is beaten in quickly until a smooth dough forms, followed by the beating in of eggs. The result is a glossy, smooth paste ready to be divided and baked. When baked, the high water content in the pastry turns to steam and forces the pastry to expand rapidly, giving it its light texture.

Hot Water Crust Pastry

Like choux pastry (paste), hot water crust pastry is a hot mixture in which water and fat (often lard) are heated to boiling point, and a flour mixture is then added. This produces a heavy but malleable dough that is then kneaded and moulded to encase meat fillings for traditional English raised pies.

Pastry Tips

When mixing a pastry or pie dough, always keep the ingredients cold, as this minimizes gluten production. Gluten is still needed to stabilize the dough, but too much will make the pastry tough.

Go easy on the dough once the liquid has been added. Overworking the dough will strengthen the gluten strands and make it less friable.

Chilling pastry and biscuit (cookie) dough not only relaxes the gluten strands of the dough, but also helps develop the flavour. It also prevents it from spreading or collapsing in the oven, and makes cookies easier to slice and bake when you want.

Always keep a hawkish eye on the oven as you approach the minimum baking time, as biscuits (cookies) will overbake in a matter of minutes. Let them cool completely before storing.

Cut shortbread while it is still warm to achieve smooth, even slices. See Shortcrust Pastry (Basic Pie Dough) for more.

Measurements & Conversions

There are many different measurement systems around the world, and even within English-speaking countries things are not always consistent: there are metric, imperial and US customary systems, all of which are widely used.

Converting different measurement systems can sometimes appear puzzling, especially because figures are always rounded for convenience. Conversion tables differ, but fret not because they will all work, as long as you stick to a single system throughout a recipe.

Most importantly, recipes are not sacred texts that can't be changed — in the history of food, recipes (or receipts, the archaic form of the word) have been altered constantly, both by top chefs and home cooks.

The following conversion tables are by no means comprehensive, but provide a useful guide to this non-exact science.

Temperature

To convert from Farenheit to Celsius, use this formula:

$$°C = (°F − 32) / 1.8$$

To convert from Celsius to Farenheit, use this formula:

$$°F = (°C \times 1.8) + 32$$

Cooking temperatures in recipes are usually given for conventional ovens. Fan (convection) ovens require slightly lower temperatures; consult the manufacturer's instructions for guidance. As a rule of thumb, set a fan (convection) oven 20°C/50°F lower than the recommended temperature.

30°C	85°F
40°C	105°F
50°C	120°F
60°C	140°F
70°C	160°F
80°C	175°F
90°C	195°F
100°C	212°F

110°C	225°F	gas mark $1/4$
120°C	250°F	gas mark $1/2$
140°C	275°F	gas mark 1
150°C	300°F	gas mark 2
160°C	325°F	gas mark 3
180°C	350°F	gas mark 4
190°C	375°F	gas mark 5
200°C	400°F	gas mark 6
220°C	425°F	gas mark 7
230°C	450°F	gas mark 8

Weight

One ounce (oz) is exactly 28.349523125 grams (g). To convert grams to ounces, just multiply by 0.0353, and to convert ounces to grams multiply by 28.3 (or by 30 to round it up). One pound (lb) is 453.59237 grams (g). To convert grams to pounds, just multiply by 0.0022, and to convert pounds to grams multiply by 453 (or 450 to round it down).

10 g	$1/3$ oz
20 g	$3/4$ oz
25 g	1 oz
50 g	2 oz

75 g	3 oz						
100 g	3 $\frac{1}{2}$ oz						
125 g	4 oz						
150 g	5 oz						
175 g	6 oz						
200 g	7 oz						
225 g	8 oz						
250 g	8 $\frac{1}{2}$ oz						
275 g	9 oz						
300 g	10 oz						
325 g	11 oz						
350 g	12 oz						
375 g	13 oz						
400 g	14 oz						
425 g	15 oz						

Metric	Equivalent
450 g	1 lb
500 g	1 lb 2 oz
1 kg	2 lb 3 $\frac{1}{2}$ oz

Volume

First of all, remember that a pint isn't always a pint! A US pint is 473 ml, while a UK imperial pint is 568 ml. When a recipe calls for teaspoon or tablespoon measurements, it refers to proper measuring spoons, which you can buy from any cookware shop (store), and are different in size from the spoons you have in your drawer. Measuring cups are also sold, to avoid confusion with all the different sizes of those used for drinking. Teaspoons and tablespoons are the same in the UK and the US, but cups are slightly different sizes.

Fluid ounces are also different in the UK and US, but not by much, so they are usually combined into one for the sake of simplification.

Remember also that volume does correspond to weight for water (so 100 ml water weighs 100 g), but not for other liquids, which have different specific weights. A pinch is said to be $\frac{1}{16}$ of a teaspoon, if you want to be pedantic, but the amount you can hold between your forefinger and thumb accurate enough.

Metric	Teaspoons	Tablespoons	Cups (UK)	Cups (US)	Fluid oz	Pints (UK)	Pints (US)
5 ml	1	$\frac{1}{3}$			$\frac{1}{6}$		
10 ml	2	$\frac{2}{3}$			$\frac{1}{3}$		
15 ml	3	1			$\frac{1}{2}$		
30 ml	6	2		$\frac{1}{8}$	1		
60 ml		4	$\frac{1}{4}$	$\frac{1}{4}$	2		
100 ml	6 $\frac{1}{2}$		$\frac{2}{5}$	$\frac{2}{5}$	3 $\frac{1}{2}$	$\frac{1}{6}$	$\frac{1}{5}$
120 ml	8			$\frac{1}{2}$	4	$\frac{1}{5}$	$\frac{1}{4}$
125 ml			$\frac{1}{2}$				
150 ml		10	$\frac{3}{5}$	$\frac{3}{5}$	5	$\frac{1}{4}$	$\frac{1}{3}$
200 ml			$\frac{4}{5}$	$\frac{4}{5}$	6 $\frac{1}{2}$	$\frac{1}{3}$	$\frac{2}{5}$
240 ml				1			$\frac{1}{2}$
250 ml			1		8 $\frac{1}{2}$	$\frac{2}{5}$	
300 ml			1 $\frac{1}{5}$	1 $\frac{1}{4}$	10	$\frac{1}{2}$	
400 ml					13 $\frac{1}{3}$		
450 ml					15		
475 ml				2			1
500 ml			2		16 $\frac{1}{2}$		
570 ml						1	
750 ml			3		25	1 $\frac{1}{3}$	1 $\frac{1}{2}$
950 ml				4	33	1 $\frac{2}{3}$	2
1 l			4		34 $\frac{1}{2}$	1 $\frac{3}{4}$	
1.15 l			4 $\frac{1}{4}$	4 $\frac{3}{4}$		2	2 $\frac{1}{2}$

Cup Conversions

Flour

These are the conversions for average plain (all-purpose) white British flour. (American flour tends to be heavier, so the conversion 1 US cup = 150 g is generally used to convert an American flour quantity into metric. Note also that wholemeal, rye and seeded flours are much heavier than white flour.) To use a cup measure accurately for dry ingredients, scoop out the ingredient from the bag rather than pouring it in and sweep off the excess with a knife to level the top. Do not press it down.

1 tbsp	9 g
$1/4$ US cup	30 g
$1/2$ US cup	65 g
1 US cup	125 g
2 US cups	250 g

Sugar

These are the conversions for granulated or caster (superfine) sugar. Brown sugar is heavier (1 US cup = 225 g), and icing (confectioners') sugar is much lighter (1 US cup = 125 g).

1 tsp	5 g
1 tbsp	15 g
$1/4$ US cup	50 g
$1/2$ US cup	100 g
1 US cup	200 g
2 US cups	400 g

Butter

These conversions also work for other solid fats, such as cheese.

Metric	Spoons and cups	Sticks
15 g	1 tbsp	$1/8$ stick
30 g	2 tbsp	$1/4$ stick
60 g	4 tbsp	$1/2$ stick
115 g	8 tbsp	1 stick
225 g	1 cup	2 sticks
450 g	2 cups	4 sticks

Length

Metric	Imperial	Metric	Imperial
5 mm	$1/4$ in	10 cm	4 in
1 cm	$2/5$ in	30 cm	1 ft
2.5 cm	1 in	50 cm	1 ft $71/2$ in
5 cm	2 in	1 m	3 ft $1/2$ in

Glossary of Terms

ALBUMEN

A technical term for egg white.

ANTICAKING AGENT

A compound added to powdered food to stop it clumping together.

BAIN-MARIE

A water-bath used to keep sauces warm and cook certain foods slowly. It can be a double boiler, a pan of boiling water with another pan or bowl on top, or a baking tin (pan) filled with water with a bowl or plate in it.

BAKE BLIND

To bake a pastry case (pie shell) without its filling, to prevent it from losing its shape. Baking beans (pie weights) are often placed on the pastry while baking.

BAKING CHOCOLATE

A type of chocolate suitable for baking, usually made from pure chocolate liquor that has been refined and mixed with a high percentage of cocoa butter (around 55%). It is usually unsweetened, but sugar is sometimes added.

BATTER

A mixture of flour, milk and eggs that is thin enough to pour.

BEURRE MANIÉ

Equal quantities of flour and softened butter stirred together and whisked in small pieces into a cooking liquid to thicken it.

BICARBONATE OF SODA

This white powder is a raising agent that, when combined with acid, produces carbon dioxide and tiny, fizzy bubbles, which expand the mixture. After the mixture is cooked, the carbon dioxide gets replaced by air resulting in a light bread or cake.

BLANCH

To immerse food in boiling water for a very short time. It helps preserve the colour in vegetables, and also helps loosen skins before peeling fruit such as peaches or tomatoes, or to help skin nuts.

BLOOD TEMPERATURE

The temperature at which liquid feels neither cold nor hot, which is close to 37°C/98.6°F.

It is also known as hand-hot temperature.

BLOOM

Bread bloom is the way the crust of the bread opens up when it is baked. Chocolate bloom refers to the dull whitish layer that can appear on the surface of chocolate due to a separation of fat or sugar. To bloom gelatine is to soak the sheets in water until they have softened.

BRAN

The hard outer layer of a grain kernel that lies below the husk. Also known as 'miller's bran', it is often a by-product of the refining process and has a high nutritional value. Wholemeal (whole-wheat) flour is about 14.5% bran.

CARAMELIZE

To heat sugar until it is melted and forms a syrup ranging in colour from golden to dark brown.

CHANTILLY

A light, sweetened, whipped cream that is flavoured with vanilla.

CLARIFY

To skim or filter a liquid to make it clear, with no impurities.

CLARIFIED BUTTER

Butter that has been heated to boiling point (so that it separates), after which the water and milk solids are removed. It is better than butter for cooking at high temperatures because the clarifying process leaves pure butter fat, which is more stable.

COULIS

A thin purée, usually of fruit mixed with a little sugar syrup, of pouring consistency. Used mainly to accompany or decorate a dish.

COUVERTURE

This fine-quality chocolate, mainly used by chefs, contains extra cocoa butter. When 'tempered' (melted, cooled and re-melted), this higher percentage of cocoa butter gives the chocolate a smooth, glossy sheen and a firmer 'snap'. Couverture is available in plain, milk and white chocolate varieties, in both blocks and chips.

CREAM

To beat a fat, usually margarine or butter, either alone or with sugar, until smooth and fluffy. This method aerates the fat and will give baked goods a lighter texture.

CRIMP

To shape the edge of pastry, either with your fingers or a fork, so that it is compressed to form folds or ridges. This ensures the pastry is sealed and gives a decorative finish.

CROQUANT

Crisp sheets of caramelized nuts and sugar, used in desserts. It is called praline when ground into a paste.

CUT IN

To distribute hard fat within the flour by cutting it using two knives in a scissor motion.

DÉTREMPE

The first step in making puff pastry. Basically a wet dough mixture of flour and water to which butter is added later.

DOT

To scatter small pieces of butter or margarine over the surface of food before cooking.

DROPPING CONSISTENCY

When a mixture is not soft enough to fall easily off the spoon but will slide off reluctantly if tapped on the side of the bowl. It should neither pour off nor continue to stick to the spoon.

DUST

To sprinkle lightly with a powder, such as icing sugar, flour or cocoa.

EGG WASH

A mixture of whisked eggs with a little water or milk that is brushed over raw dough or pastry before baking to glaze it or help it stick together.

FAN (CONVECTION) OVEN

A fan-assisted electric or gas oven that circulates heat evenly around the oven with a fan. This allows for a faster baking time when using several oven racks at a time.

FÉCULE

A starch, such as potato starch or cornflour.

FEUILLETÉ(E)

Meaning 'flaky' and used to describe a puff pastry case.

FOLD

To mix food gently from the bottom of a bowl to the top with the help of a spatula or spoon. To fold ingredients properly, the heavier ingredient is placed at the bottom of the bowl and the lighter one on top.

GANACHE

A rich icing made from chocolate and cream that is heated and stirred together until the chocolate melts. The mixture is then cooled until lukewarm and applied onto a cake for a satin finish.

GELATINE

A product derived from the bones of animals and used as a setting agent for sweet or savoury jellies and pudding fillings. It comes in the form of sheets, powder or granules. Alternative substitutes to gelatine are agar-agar, which is obtained from seaweed, and pectin, which comes fom ripe fruit.

GILD

To add a glaze of beaten egg or egg yolk before baking in order to give a shiny colour to the surface of the food.

GLAZE

A sweet or savoury glossy liquid coating applied to baked goods for shine, flavour and colour.

GLUTEN

A protein found in cereal grains, particularly wheat. It is a sticky substance that is vital for bread making, as it keeps dough stretchy and flexible and helps it to rise.

GREASE

To spread cooking fat on the surface of a dish, tin or pan to prevent sticking.

KNEAD

To fold, push and turn a stiff dough to give it a smooth texture.

KNOCK BACK/PUNCH DOWN

To punch or press a yeasted dough once or twice after proving (proofing) so as to remove any large air pockets that may have formed. The dough is then allowed to prove (proof) again for an even crumb structure, and is then baked.

LIAISON

A mixture of egg yolks and heavy cream that is used to thicken a sauce. It can also refer to other thickening agents, such as cornflour, a roux or beurre manié.

LIGHTEN

To incorporate air into a dish by carefully folding in lightly whipped cream or egg whites, for instance.

LINE

To cover the bottom sides of a pan, mould or terrine with a thin layer of greaseproof paper, strips of bacon or thin slices of cake in order to stop a filling sticking or to hold in a soft filling.

MERINGUE

A mixture of whipped egg whites and sugar. There are two basic types of meringues: hard meringues are baked at a low temperature for several hours until dry and crisp on the outside and sticky on the inside, whereas soft meringues are moist and tender and are used for topping desserts.

MISE EN PLACE

The culinary procedures that take place before service starts in a professional kitchen, such as chopping vegetables and preparing sauces.

MOUNT

To emulsify a sauce with cold butter to give it texture, flavour and shine. Also the act of whipping cream or eggs.

NATURAL LEAVEN/ SOURDOUGH STARTER

A mixture of flour and water left to ferment with naturally occurring yeasts and used to make leavened breads.

OVEN-SPRING

The initial burst of rising when a yeast-leavened bread first enters the oven. The blast of heat stimulates the yeast and increases fermentation, before killing off the yeast at 60°C/140°F.

PANADE

A thick mixture of flour, butter, milk or water and sometimes eggs which is used as the base of soufflés and choux pastry.

PETITS FOURS

Bite-sized cakes and pastries.

PIPE

To force a mixture through a nozzle in order to cover or decorate a surface.

PRE-FERMENT

A portion of dough that has been allowed to ferment before being incorporated with the final dough, and which helps the bread rise and strengthens the dough structure and quality. Also known as a starter. The common pre-ferments are poolish, biga, sponge, sourdough starter and fermented dough.

PROVE (PROOF)

To leave the dough to rise for the second time after it has been shaped, usually to double its initial size.

QUENELLE

A small oval-shaped portion of any sweet or savoury cream, mousse or purée, which can be served as a garnish or on its own.

QUICK BREAD

A type of bread that has been leavened by non-yeast leavening agents, such as soda bread.

REST

To set a dough aside to allow the gluten strands to relax. This intermission makes it easier for the dough to be rolled out and shaped later. The dough should be covered to prevent it from drying out.

RIBBON STAGE

A stage in which the egg yolk and sugar mixture forms a slowly disappearing ribbon pattern on the surface of the mixture when some of it is lifted.

ROYAL ICING

A soft paste made from whisked egg whites, icing sugar and lemon juice that dries to a smooth, hard finish. It is traditionally used for frosting dense cakes such as wedding and Christmas cakes, but also for intricate piping of decorations.

RUB IN

To integrate butter or margarine into flour by rubbing them together with the fingertips until the mixture resembles breadcrumbs.

SCORE

To make slashes in the surface of the dough just before baking, primarily to prevent the loaf from tearing at weak spots.

SEIZE

When melting chocolate, to curdle or turn thick and grainy when it comes into contact with water or overheats. To salvage this, add 1 tablespoon of fat (such as vegetable oil, cocoa butter or clarified butter) per 170 g/6 oz of chocolate and stir gently.

SEMOLINA

A coarse flour ground from hard durum wheat and used to make traditional pasta, bread, pizza and biscuit doughs. It can be used to flour baking surfaces as an alternative to corn meal.

SETTING POINT

The stage at which a mixture containing gelatine starts to set. The temperature at this stage is 104°C/220°F.

SLAKE

To mix a powder with a small amount of liquid to form a paste so that it can be mixed into a larger amount of liquid without forming lumps.

SOFT PEAKS

The peaks that form after egg whites have been beaten and which quickly collapse when the beaters are lifted up. You beat egg whites to this stage when folding them into a batter and before adding sugar.

STIFF PEAKS

The peaks that form after egg whites have been beaten and which hold their shape after lifting the beaters. They occur after sugar has been added and are used to make meringue biscuits (cookies), for instance.

STRONG WHITE FLOUR

This flour is made from hard wheat (or a mixture of hard and soft wheat), which contains a grain with a higher gluten content. It is therefore ideal for breadmaking so as to ensure strong, stretchy gluten that will hold lots of air bubbles.

TEMPER

To heat and cool melted chocolate to specific temperatures to harden it into a crystalline structure that gives it sheen and a pleasing snap without any graininess. This is done through melting and cooling the chocolate in a controlled way.

THREAD STAGE

An early stage of sugar syrup boiling. To test it, drop a bit of the syrup into cold water and then pull between your fingers: at 110°C/225°F it should form a liquid thread as it is pulled.

VEGETABLE SHORTENING

A vegetarian alternative to lard, this is a solid fat made from hydrogenated vegetable oils, such as cottonseed and soybean oil. It is often used in baking and for basting meat.

WHITE CHOCOLATE

Strictly not real chocolate since it does not contain any cocoa solids, being made primarily of cocoa butter, sugar and milk solids. White chocolate must contain at least 20% cocoa butter and 14% total milk solids, including 3.5% milk fat.